Fair Trade as Christian Mission

Chris Sugden

Director of Academic Affairs,
Oxford Centre for Mission Studies

GW00640701

GROVE BOOKS LIMITED
RIDLEY HALL RD CAMBRIDGE CB3 9HU

Contents

Acknowledgements

This booklet is dedicated to all those who make up the Traidcraft community of purpose, a number of around 200,000 producers and their families, Fair Traders and their customers, mail order customers, staff, shareholders and donors.

The booklet originated in a workshop at a Traidcraft National Conference. I am grateful to present and past members of the Traidcraft Foundation, Peter Johnson, Roger Hird, and Deryke Belshaw, and to Stuart Raistrick, chairman of Traidcraft plc Board, Philip Angier, managing director of Traidcraft plc, Graham Young, Director of Traidcraft Exchange and Derek Malin, Traidcraft Fair Trader, for their helpful comments and input. However, the booklet is not a statement of Traidcraft policy. It reflects on the practical experience of engaging with these questions with Traidcraft. It also draws on a 1997 Durham University dissertation by Judith Sugden which investigates the history and efficacy of Traidcraft and the Fair Trade movement in achieving their objectives.[1] But the views expressed in this booklet are only those of the author in a private capacity.

There are other fair trade organizations in the UK—Oxfam Trading, Tearcraft, Equal Exchange, Twin Trading. Other organizations seek to develop business enterprise in the two-thirds world— Opportunity International and Shared Interest. This study focuses on one organization in the spirit of the principle of incarnation, by looking at a practical expression rather than leaving discussion at the level of speculative theory. I hope that both those engaged in fair trade and those concerned for Christian mission will find some value and encouragement in this consideration of the basis of both.

Finally my thanks to the members of the Grove Ethics Group for their encouragement and input.

1   *Is there a fair trade model that can be extended to International Trade at a Macro-Level?* by Judith Sugden (Durham University, BA Dissertation in Combined Studies for Social Sciences, 1997).

The Cover Illustration is by Peter Ashton

Copyright © Chris Sugden 1999

First Impression April 1999
ISSN 0951-2659
ISBN 1 85174 399 5

1

Introduction

Traidcraft is a Christian response to poverty. It was founded in 1979 as a work done in obedience to and dependence on God. It has sought to address poverty in a Christian way because it believes that Christian faith and practice can and should make a difference to the way we engage in trade. It is a Christian attempt to demonstrate that it is possible to engage as a trading company in the market place and also ensure a fair deal for those from the two-thirds world who are seeking to sell their products in the international market.[2] In 1999 the commercial trading arm, Traidcraft plc, has a turnover of eight million pounds and generates approximately two million days employment in the two-thirds world for 100 producer groups comprising 80,000 producers and their dependents. Alongside the PLC, Traidcraft Exchange, a charity, provides business development expertise to two-thirds world producers and input on issues of fair trade to government, business and education. Traidcraft also pioneered and set up Shared Interest as a savings scheme that enables people to make their savings available as loans to two-thirds world producers. It also pioneered social accounting as a means of evaluating a company's performance that goes beyond the 'bottom line.' Traidcraft traces a path between the breakfast table of the consumer and the breakfast table of the producer, and is involved in all the steps along that path.

I have been privileged to be a Trustee of the Traidcraft Foundation—the charity which has a controlling interest in the PLC and Traidcraft Exchange—since 1985, and to be its current chairman. Traidcraft has followed the life-cycle of many organizations—birth, childhood insecurity, adolescence trying various possibly productive activities, young adulthood taking part in giving birth to other organizations (such as Shared Interest) and even a mid-life crisis of re-evaluating its objectives and goals. It seeks to be an intentional community of interest, comprising staff, shareholders, over 4000 voluntary representatives (now called Fair Traders), and producers and producers' organizations in the two-thirds world.

Traidcraft was established by Christians and seeks to encapsulate Christian values and principles in its work. This booklet addresses questions raised by such a combination of fair trade business and Christian mission. Some Christians cannot see what fair trade has to do with them. Other Christians ask whether Traidcraft sufficiently stresses the Christian aspects of its mission. Others with a passionate commitment to fair trade ask what Christian faith contributes to fighting poverty through trade.

One of the originating impulses of Traidcraft was that poverty is no respecter of a person's religion. Traidcraft seeks to help poor people of whatever religious

---

2   The history is written by Richard Adams in *Who Profits: A Revealing Case Study in Successful Trading with Developing Countries* (Oxford: Lion Publishing, 1989).

persuasion. It also welcomes partnership with those who do not share its Christian commitments, yet it requires its trustees, boards and senior staff to affirm their commitment to Christian principles. How then may we understand Christian work with those who do not share Christian convictions in Christian mission? These issues are faced by other and older Christian mission and service organizations such as church schools where Christians work alongside those who share many of their commitments but not their faith. This discussion may hopefully be of interest to them as well.

2

What is Fair Trade?

Judith Sugden writes:
> The 'Fair Trade' movement was started by individuals who recognized the outcomes of international market activity as 'unfair' (unjust, biased and inequitable). An understanding of this situation as being the responsibility of the industrialized countries, a concern for the welfare of those producers reduced to poverty and dependent on aid, and an awareness of the importance of international trade to these producers, led to the setting up of 'alternative' trading organizations. The first ATOs were 'world shops' opened in the Netherlands at the end of the 1960s…The shops sold third world products, usually kept out of the European market by heavy import duties, and charged the consumer slightly more for them. Since many ATOs started up independently across the world during the 1960s there is no formal set of principles that can be identified as 'fair trade.' The concept of fair trade is worked out in practice rather than rigid principles as trading organizations work with the producers to address what they need and want. In this respect, 'fair trade' is a grass roots approach to the problems of trade, an approach much advocated in current development theory…In all cases the main concern is that those in the third world are able to gain from participation in trade rather than be subject to it.[3]

Four main principles have been recognized as constituting a 'fair trade' relationship between trading partners:
- A direct relationship with the poor producer—so fair trade seeks to direct help to the most disadvantaged.
- A fair price should be given to the producer for their product so that they are not at the mercy of the vagaries of the international market.

---

3 Judith Sugden, *Is there a Fair Trade model?* p 34.

- Credit is available in advance of the receipt of goods, providing important access to credit for those who are denied it.
- A long-term partnership with the producer.

These principles must be understood in the context of what constitutes 'unfairness' in trade. Part of the problem of trade is the uncertainty and risk in markets. The poorest are the most vulnerable to this problem. Large international producers can diversify their products to absorb difficulties experienced in one area. Poor producers are often stuck with one product and one outlet. They are therefore denied many of the advantages and the protection of international trade. In the context of such 'unfairness' of the market to such poor producers, the four main principles have been an attempt to move towards greater fairness and a more level playing field.

'A *direct relationship* between the ATO and the producer...means that more money is received by the producer...It brings producer welfare (otherwise obscured by the many intermediaries) to the attention of the supplier and also the consumer. It is also an efficient way of directing help to the most disadvantaged producers...When directed solely through governments and intermediaries, mismanagement usually results in a significant waste of resources.'

'A *fair price* agreed on by producer and buyer is one of the most recognized practices embodied in fair trade. It means that producers no longer suffer from low prices on the international market.'[4] The price producers receive is above the world market price, so that even if world prices fall, the price producers involved with fair trade receive is still sufficient for their needs.

The *advance payment* of the fair price to the producer provides them with the resources needed to meet the order given and also serves to allow investment in resources for diversification. These credit terms give the producer fifty per cent of the payment before receipt of the order and thus provide easy access to credit. Such credit access has a significant impact on the welfare of the poor.

The *long-term partnership* between producer and buyer guarantees a market for a specific quantity of goods for a specific period. This provides them with security and enables them to plan ahead.

These four principles have shaped the movement but are not always advocated now with equal strength. Some argue that fair price and advance credit are of greater weight than direct relationships and long-term partnerships. In future some ATOs will probably develop specialisms in particular goods and supply other ATOs, thus ending the direct relationship between producer and each ATO that sells their goods. What matters to poor producers is access to markets. The concern to cut out middle people was to ensure that the producer received as much benefit from the sale of the product as possible. Traidcraft itself has developed a 'middleman' role by developing Shared Interest to assist producers in accessing finance to develop their businesses. As the fair trade market matures,

4   *Is there a Fair Trade model?* pp 35–37.

ATOs are themselves becoming middle people. If the development of specialist ATOs means a larger market share for poor producers, then some would advocate taking that route in the long term interests of the producers.

Other Features of ATOs

ATOs work with both consumers and producers. Judith Sugden writes: 'ATOs work with *small scale producer groups* who meet particular criteria concerning member relations and welfare. They encourage environmentally sustainable production techniques and provide training skills. They work to educate the consumers of the product as well as campaigning at a government level...All these measures directly address and work to overcome the difficulties that participation in international trade can pose for the poorest producers.'[5] ATOs usually look for trading partners that are *small scale operations.* Agricultural producer groups for smallholders are the largest category of primary producers. It is through small producer groups that grass roots development can take place.[6]

For producer groups to become fair trading partners they must affirm and express basic human rights, as laid out by the United Nations Universal Declaration of Human Rights. These are rights to 'decent wages, adequate living conditions, worker representation, minimum health and safety standards' (Traidcraft Foundation Principles). These rights do not exist somewhere as a template to be imposed. They represent an aspiration towards greater human flourishing.[7]

Producer welfare, often not an issue in trade, becomes a priority in fair trade. Members of a producer group or co-operative should take part in decision-making. Social benefits provided for members can involve health and education projects run for the local community. Conditions concerning the workplaces must be met, as laid down by international agreement.

'The encouragement of *environmentally sustainable products and production methods* combats increasing environmental degradation...Instead of suffering declining yields and destruction of their subsistence base, producers within fair trade actually increase their yield and the value of it through organic farming and selective collection of raw materials (eg wood for craft products).'[8]

'Many ATOs *provide information* about the international market as well as training and advice in business organization, techniques, design and skills to enable the producers to benefit from that knowledge and successfully enter the export market. Without this help poor producers cannot compete on the same level as other exporters and they do not have the resources to invest in such support themselves. Their success in the market depends on meeting consumer preferences for style and quality, and their very entry into the market can be determined by the standards set for imports by certain non-tariff barriers.'

5 *Is there a Fair Trade model?* p 38.
6 *Op cit,* p 38.
7 See further Chris Sugden, *The Right to be Human* (Grove Ethical Studies No 102, Cambridge: 1997).
8 *Is there a Fair Trade model?* p 40.

'*Education of consumers* about the consequences of unfair trade, and campaigns against tariffs and other trade barriers at national and international levels, seek to work towards consumer pressure for a more widespread adoption of fair trade by trading organizations and governments. Information about the producers of the products sold serves to bring their welfare to consumer attention and highlight the part that consumers themselves can play in alleviating poverty... Campaigning at a political level raises the profile of these disadvantaged producers and is a recognized course of action among NGOs seeking to alleviate poverty.'[9]

The cancellation of debts of two-thirds world countries will not itself address the immediate problems of poverty their people face. Poor producers ultimately need markets, and an alternative market hopes to guarantee that for them. Alternative trading organizations bring ethical products to the consumer in a way which widens consumer choice.

'Fair trade can therefore be seen as fitting the description of a "blend of market-based economy, social justice and environmental factors," as it works towards bringing producers into an alternative trading market in an attempt to reduce poverty...Social justice is fundamental to the fair trade approach...There are [two] different conceptions of social justice. One is concerned with the "end-state" and the other requires that the "process of exchange between individuals should be controlled and checked in accordance with abstract, external moral principles." Fair trade addresses both.'[10] It influences behaviour in the market place, making it less likely that the differentials (market power, information and human capital) between producers and buyers are exploited, because the outcomes of trade are seen as unsatisfactory. Fair trade has only moral not legislative authority. 'Fair trade is also an enactment of social justice, in response to human need, where needs can be understood as health care, educational opportunity etc.'[11]

The market system may be able to satisfy consumer wants but is not always able to satisfy producer needs. The protection of industrialized markets prevented private businesses in third world economies from making gains. Given that the international market system offers the opportunity for all to benefit, fair trade's advocacy of a fair trading relationship between producers and consumers as a corrective measure demonstrates some of the neo-liberal confidence in the market mechanism.

Traidcraft is one such ATO. Its current mission statement is as follows:

'Traidcraft's Mission is to fight poverty through trade.

Traidcraft's goal is to double its impact by the year 2002. Signs of Traidcraft's success will be: Improving the livelihoods of "third-world" producers; providing effective local support for producers; setting trends in ethical business; winning more customers and supporters; leading opinion in the fair trade movement.

Traidcraft is a Christian response to poverty. It strives to show a bias to the poor;

9 *Is there a Fair Trade model?* p 41.
10 *Op cit*, p 43.
11 *Op cit*, p 43.

respect people and the environment; be transparent and accountable; show creativity and innovation; be the best.'

Traidcraft's experience since November 1979 is that providing an alternative market for some producers is not enough, nor sufficiently commercially viable as a business venture. Producers require help in accessing the mainstream international market. Traidcraft therefore developed a Partner Development and Product Marketing Service, and joined in developing a Fair Trade Mark Scheme, the Ethical Trading Initiative and Shared Interest to provide access to credit.

All this may effectively help the poor. But how does it express Christian mission? The next sections will reflect first on the Bible in the light of that question, and then reflect on the activity of Traidcraft and ATOs in the light of the Bible.

3
How Did Jesus Engage in Mission?

Jesus is the pattern for our mission. When he appeared to the disciples on Easter evening in the locked upper room, he said that 'As the Father sent me, so send I you' (John 20.21). The pattern for Jesus' mission was to announce and demonstrate the kingdom of God.

Mark 1.14 introduces and summarizes Jesus' ministry as announcing that 'the kingdom of God has drawn near.' Matthew 10.5–8 records Jesus' commission to the disciples to 'proclaim the good news: The kingdom of heaven has come near. Cure the sick, raise the dead, cleanse the lepers, cast out demons.' The kingdom of God fulfils God's purposes in creation. It will come in its fullness when Jesus returns and brings history to its climax. It is where God's will is done 'on earth as it is in heaven.' Jesus announced that the reality (but not full extent) of the kingdom had come to earth through his ministry. His mission is therefore about more than personal relationships. It is about enabling God's will to be done in all areas of human activity in managing the creation. Proclaiming the good news of the kingdom involved word and deed. For example, Luke 8.1–3 records that Jesus went through cities and villages proclaiming and bringing the good news of the kingdom of God. Luke adds that both the disciples and a number of women went around with him. This was an extraordinary demonstration of the kingdom they were proclaiming. For it was against Jewish tradition and custom for men and women to mix freely in public. These women included people from different social 'strata.' The men could not have done their work without these many women who provided for Jesus and the disciples out of their resources. So Jesus' kingdom activity demonstrated God's will in the arena of male/female relationships.

Good News to the Poor

Jesus ministry, was to bring 'good news to the poor' (Luke 4.18). In the Bible, the term 'poor' means what it means in common sense English—the economically and socially disadvantaged. When John the Baptist sent his messengers to Jesus to find if he is the one to come or whether they should look for someone else, Jesus answered 'Go and tell John what you have seen and heard: the blind receive their sight, the lame walk, the lepers are cleansed, the deaf hear, the dead are raised, the poor have good news brought to them' (Luke 7.22). Jesus is referring to those whose physical conditions in life are of deprivation and suffering when he refers to the blind, the lame, the lepers, the deaf and the dead—and the poor. An international biblical study concluded 'The poor (in Scripture) refers to the manual worker who struggles to survive on a day to day basis, the destitute cowering as a beggar, the one reduced to meekness, the one brought low...those weak and tired from carrying heavy burdens, and very often the common people.'[12] The 'poor in spirit' refers to those who because of their condition in this world are dependent on or have turned to God. The term does not refer to spiritual deadness, atheism or humility. For many poor people the good news of Jesus has been that in societies where they are marginalized and treated as 'nobodies,' they have an identity as children of God through the free grace of God in Jesus.

What then is the good news to the poor? It is that God has established his kingdom of righteousness and peace through the incarnation, ministry, atoning death and resurrection of his Son Jesus Christ. The kingdom fulfils God's purpose in creation by bringing wholeness to humanity and the whole creation. In the kingdom, people receive by grace alone a new status before God and people, a new dignity and worth as his daughters and sons, and empowerment by his Spirit to be stewards of creation and servants of one another in a new community. The kingdom will come in its fullness in a new heaven and earth only when Jesus returns.

Those who respond to this good news who are poor in the material sense or powerless are empowered by the Spirit and served by other members of the kingdom community to experience full humanity as stewards of God's creation. The non-poor who become poor-in-spirit receive a true dignity replacing false pride in riches and are liberated to be truly human with a passion for justice for the poor. They are to trust in the power of God's Spirit which enables them to serve rather than to control. They enter a new family that accepts them for who they are rather than for their achievements—in material prosperity or status. The task of evangelization among the majority of the unreached who are poor will be carried out primarily by those who are poor, with appropriate support from those economically advantaged who are poor in spirit.'[13]

---

1 2 *Christian Witness to the Urban Poor* published by the Lausanne Committee for World Evangelization from their consultation in Thailand in 1980; reproduced in *Evangelism and the Poor* edited by Vinay Samuel and Chris Sugden (Exeter: Paternoster, 1982).

13 Report of the Social Concern Track of Lausanne II at Manila, June 1989, published in *Transformation* July 1990. Also in *AD 2000 and Beyond—A Mission Agenda* edited by Vinay Samuel and Chris Sugden (Oxford: Regnum, 1991).

Jesus sought what can be called the 'frontier' of the good news of the kingdom with the situation of different groups of people as he met them. For each group of people, the question we could imagine Jesus asking was 'If the kingdom of God came tomorrow morning, what would change most significantly for this group of people?' Jesus took the Pharisees to task for concentrating on the petty details of the law to the exclusion of its real concerns for justice, mercy and peace (Matt 23.23). The law had been given to Israel to ensure that the injustice that they had experienced in Pharaoh's Egypt was not repeated in the promised land. It was given 'that there will be no one in need among you' (Deut 15.4). But the Pharisees turned the law into a means of excluding people they described as 'sinners' from the society of Israel. For the sick, the most significant change was to their fatalism. They were led to believe that they were under God's curse and that nothing could be done for them. Jesus tells those he heals that their faith has healed them (Matt 9.22, Mk 5.34, Mk 10.52).

The Fulfilment of Creation

The kingdom of God fulfils God's purposes in creation. The New Testament looks forward to the time when the kingdoms of this world have become the kingdom of our Lord (Rev 11.15), and when the kings of the earth bring the glory of the nations into the city of God (Rev 21.24). The kingdom of God when Jesus returns will mean a new heaven and a new earth where righteousness will be at home (Rev 21.1).

One of God's purposes in creation was that men and women together would be stewards of the creation. The meaning of the term 'image of God' (Genesis 1.27–28) is that humanity images or represents the invisible God who owns the earth as his manager and tenant. God commands those who image him to be fruitful and have dominion over the earth on his behalf. This dominion is not unrestrained tyranny; it is to mirror the dominion of God, who in Scripture is a caring shepherd king. All should be stewards of creation. Stewardship requires access to resources. Lack of access to useful and productive work undermines people's humanity. An increasing awareness by individuals of their responsibilities as stewards is seen in their ability to take responsibility for decisions, and to use resources efficiently. All who are responsible for the stewardship of creation should also receive the fruits of creation. This stewardship in Genesis is set in the context of the family, of the command to men and women to be fruitful and multiply.

The fall has impaired our ability to be stewards. The corruption of the relationships between people and between people and the environment is an expression of the corruption of their relationship with God.

God's action to bring salvation to the world began with poor Hebrew migrant slaves in Egypt. He delivered them and gave them a land, and a law to live by. The law's purpose was that the oppression of Pharaoh's Egypt should not obtain among them. But, recognizing the reality of poverty, as of divorce, the law made provisions for loans for the poor. A zero-interest loan was available, and if the principal was not repaid by the end of six years, the balance would be forgiven

(Ex 22.25; Lev 25.35–38; Dt 15.1–11). John Mason comments:

The biblical provision of a compassionate loan provides assistance to the able-bodied without either unnecessarily stigmatizing them or creating conditions ripe for excessive dependency upon assistance programmes. A loan recognizes that the weaker family unit remains a productive component of the community which can, with time and some reduced consumption, very probably take care of its economic responsibilities. Use of a loan protects against the development of excessive dependence upon assistance. A loan requires less community concern to monitor; the loan obligation serves as a pressure to work harder rather than to shirk. The compassionate aspects of the loan indicate the community's acknowledgement that the weaker family had little control over its difficulties, and that the community is willing to assist. (So) it is good for the social-psychological health of the adversely affected *beth'ab* [father's house].[14]

Implicit in this provision is the concern that people should be protected in their ability to be stewards of the creation. Part of our expression of salvation in this world should involve the demonstration of the recovery of our responsibility for creation and should enable people to recover their position as managers of creation. Paul indicates that God's purpose is that Christian disciples be 'conformed to the image of [God's] Son' (Rom 8.29). Jesus is the second Adam, the true image of God, the true steward of the earth, the one who shows us how to manage the earth. Disciples of Jesus should know and show how to manage the earth best. When God's purpose is fulfilled, the kings of the earth will bring the glory of the nations into the city of God (Rev 21.22). The best of humanity's stewardship will be present in the new earth—transformed but recognizable. In obeying God's will for humanity, we should also seek to enable human beings to be stewards and managers of creation. And this purpose will find fulfilment in the new heaven and new earth.

Thus Christian mission is reversing the effects of the fall. It points up the integral effects of human sin in distorting all people's relationships, demonstrates the nature of a right relationship with God in restoring stewardship and shows the necessity of a relationship with Christ so that people be servants of one another. It demonstrates the nature of sin, the nature of God redeeming creation, and points to the need for allegiance to Christ.

In obedience to a biblical understanding of mission, Christian mission throughout the two-thirds world has been a response to the needs of the whole person to be treated with dignity, to exercise stewardship and to be able to support the family. The very start of the nineteenth century mission activity of the western churches in Africa was to repay the debt to Africa incurred by the slave trade. According to the president of the World Bank, James Wolfensohn, the current standing of the Christian church is that it is *de facto* the world's largest Non-Governmental Organization, and according to the World Health Organization, the

---

14 John Mason 'Assistance Programmes in the Bible' *Transformation* April 1987, pp 3–5.

church is the world's largest provider of health care. It reaches into almost every village on earth.

Sharing the Gospel

The gospel is shared in many ways in Scripture. I want to highlight two. First, Jesus shared the gospel with those who were 'outsiders' through parables. Jesus says 'To you [disciples] has been given the secret of the kingdom of God, but for those outside everything comes in parables, in order that "they may indeed look, but not perceive, and may indeed listen, but not understand"' (Mk 4.10–12). I suggest that *the parable is a form of communication particularly suited to those who do not want to hear.* The classic parable is that which Nathan told King David (2 Sam 12). Imagine Nathan's problem. The King of Israel had both committed adultery with Bathsheba and murdered her husband by proxy. Anyone who openly rebuked David would have a sharply decreased life expectancy. Nathan constructed a drama in which David had to make a judgment. He flattered David by explaining a problem to him, of the man with many flocks who stole a poor man's one ewe lamb to prepare a meal for a guest. David pronounced that 'the man who has done this deserves to die.' David committed himself. He could not turn back. Nathan only had to say 'You are the man.' Jesus' parables create a drama in which the listeners are asked to make a judgment. They find that they have judged themselves and cannot turn back. They will never be the same again. They do not come to faith at once—but they have gone one step along the road.

The gospel is also shared in Scripture through *event and explanation.* An event takes place which someone gets up to explain. When the Spirit comes on the Day of Pentecost, the disciples appear on the streets of Jerusalem speaking all the languages of the Mediterranean. How can this be explained? Some suggest that they are drunk. Peter explains that Jesus has been raised by God and sent his Spirit in fulfilment of the prophecy of Joel. In Acts 3 the same process happens. Peter and John heal a lame man at the Beautiful Gate of the temple. He runs into the temple praising God. Peter explains that this marvel was through Jesus whom they crucified and God raised from the dead. Peter and John get arrested, but only to get the chance for giving a further explanation, this time to the very Jewish rulers who had had Jesus put to death a few weeks earlier.

Thus one pattern of Jesus is to announce and demonstrate the kingdom of God, which fulfils God's purposes in creation and particularly focuses on the poor, in ways that are relevant to each group and stimulate them to make a judgment and seek an explanation. We will now examine how Christian involvement in fair trade expresses this pattern.

4
How Traidcraft Expresses Christian Mission

The activities of Traidcraft faithfully express some of these biblical patterns today. Judith Sugden writes: 'Fair trade is not a general theory of trade…Fair trade is…a pragmatic response to unsatisfactory outcomes of the market by changing the nature of trading relationships…The fact there is no theory (of fair trade) indicates the essential pragmatism of fair trade.'[15]

Fair trade has been a grass roots movement—not one born of precepts brought down from above. It has been a response of practical compassion often rooted in a Christian worldview that refuses to accept that in the market the only categories are winners and losers. The concept of fair trade is worked out as trading organizations work with the poor producers to address what they need and want. It is a grass roots approach to express a concern that those in the two-thirds world gain from participation in trade rather than be subject to it.

Judith Sugden argues that the point of fair trade is that (poor) producers' (legitimate and just) interests are met. An approach that addresses producer interests and needs from the grass roots out of a concern for social justice has extremely positive results in terms of poverty alleviation, social development and extending the producer interests into the mainstream.[16]

Poor producers need markets. Fair trade organizations have provided a niche market, and placed a premium on products as the volume of fairly traded goods is too small to benefit from economies of scale. But poor producers need help in accessing the mainstream international market within a framework which ensures they are not exploited. They are not there just to challenge consumer's consciences. The increase in the fair trade movement has encouraged many poor producers whose primary need is access to the market. Poor producer interests can be met by enabling them to enter the international market through business development, credit schemes, labelling and the development of ethical trading. This goes beyond the role of Alternative Trading Organizations.

What ATOs can achieve is limited. In 1990 the estimated annual earnings of ATOs were £250 million; the income of Tate and Lyle, one international trader in sugar, was £3,432 million. But 'by acting as prototypes for the new initiatives, [ATOs] demonstrate to other trading companies that fair trade principles can be applied to all aspects of the market and are viable within it.'[17] The activities of ATOs can have an influence out of all proportion to their size. Traidcraft has provided considerable input to the Labour Party's policy on the role of business in international development, and the British Government White Paper on International

15 *Is there a Fair Trade model?* p 66.
16 *Op cit*, pp 71–2.
17 *Op cit*, p 70.

Development. But that input depends on it putting those principles to the test in its own business.

Traidcraft has grown as a grassroots prophetic movement seeking justice, offering prototypes for new initiatives in trading and business relationships. This follows the pattern of Christian involvement in medicine and education. Christians were often the first to begin schools and hospitals and are often still the first to do so in poor and remote areas. Other people of good will saw the contribution of their work. In time other organizations and governments themselves took on the responsibility of providing universal access to education and health. The response of Christians has been twofold: first, to take their own place in the new national institutions; second, to pioneer new areas. Thus in the UK Health Service, Christians pioneered the Hospice Movement which is now gaining similar wide acceptance.

How do the activities of Traidcraft express some of these biblical patterns today?

Biblical Patterns in Practice

First, *Traidcraft's work in seeking justice through trade, is a frontier of the kingdom with the current economic order.* What would the world economic order look like if the kingdom of God came tomorrow morning? There would be justice in exchange and trade. If God's final kingdom of peace and righteousness will be marked by justice and that kingdom has entered the world already in Jesus, then we are called to show signs of the kingdom at the frontiers with rebellious human society. Working for justice through trade demonstrates what the kingdom looks like when it encounters the injustice of the world economic trading systems. This signpost points in turn to Jesus Christ, whose resurrection assures us that this kingdom will one day finally triumph.

Secondly, *Traidcraft activities act as a kind of parable.* If we were to knock on people's front doors and explain that the poverty of the poor was intimately linked with them, many would probably give us no more than a ten second hearing. A Traidcraft stall and Traidcraft goods draw people in rather like a parable. They come, perhaps, out of a sense of compassion for those who suffer. We encourage them to purchase goods made in the two-thirds world, and with the educational backup suggest that it is not so much compassion for those who suffer as justice for those who are wronged. One Fair Trader told me how someone had come to her stall in church one day with friends and commented 'I wouldn't have those apricots if I were you, they have been touched by brown hands.' An embarrassed silence fell. It was clear to everyone, and finally to the shopper herself, that she had passed a judgment on herself. Traidcraft's parabolic ministry moves people one step forward. They can never be the same again.

Thirdly, *Traidcraft is an event with an explanation.* The event is the event of a Traidcraft sale. The explanation is why we should purchase goods from the two-thirds world, often at a higher price than in the supermarkets. The explanation is about justice and fairness—about why buy from such groups and communities.

The ultimate answer is because the reality of the universe is shown in Jesus who shows that the Lord of the world is a Lord of justice and mercy whose will is that all have the opportunity to manage the earth.

Fourthly, *Traidcraft opens up a relationship between the poor and the non-poor.* Many analyses of poverty and prescriptions for dealing with it set the poor in conflict with the non-poor. In Christian terms it is the work of evil (the principalities and powers) to create division out of difference, whether in race, gender, class or material resources. The work of Jesus Christ is to break down the barriers between separated and hostile groups. This is the clear teaching of Ephesians 2–3. The dwelling place of the Holy Spirit is a community where such barriers have been broken. Jesus spoke of the destructive power of mammon in people's lives. It is a rival divinity to God, which leads people to get their priorities wrong, and prevents them from entering God's kingdom where they would find fulfilment of their humanity. It blinds people to the needs of others. To enter the kingdom people need to renounce wealth (Mark 10.27); love for riches is a major obstacle to spiritual growth (Mark 4.19), and fields, oxen and marriage arrangements lead people to refuse God's invitation. The cross made community between hostile groups possible. So the reaction of biblical Christians to those different from themselves should be to seek partnership. Vinay Samuel points out 'Because the prime categories [are] those saved by Christ and those as yet unsaved, the biblical Christian does not think of rich and poor as the primary divisions or categories. The understanding the poor has of the rich is not of a powerful oppressor, but of a person. The evangelical never feels powerless against the rich. He or she still feels he or she has the gospel to share. The slum dweller may lack much, but has the priceless treasure of Christ, the hope of glory. Therefore the poor need never accept the rich as people who cannot change. They can confidently, not arrogantly, share something with the rich that the rich need.'[18]

In the process of this sharing the rich also can develop a new basis for their identity—the grace of God in Christ. In the parable of the rich fool, Jesus teaches that riches blind people to the kingdom of God because rich people tend to seek their identity and security in wealth. That approach leads to endless anxiety and worry. Jesus encourages people to seek their security in the kingdom of God, in the care of the heavenly Father who provides for the birds and the flowers. God will provide the basic necessities of life for his subjects. So they have no need to use up their energy worrying about their future, persecution or death. Instead, free of self-concern they can attend to God's kingdom standards for just relationships. Since God will provide their necessities, members in the kingdom can give to the poor.

Giving to the poor is saving up treasure in heaven (Luke 12.33) and enables trust in God to be expressed. Jesus points out that people are to seek first the kingdom of God, and everything else will be added to them. Once people seek

---

18 Vinay Samuel quoted in Chris Sugden 'Jesus Christ, Saviour and Liberator' in Nicholls and Wood (eds), *Sharing Good News with the Poor* (Carlisle: Paternoster, 1996).

their security in the right place, they are freed from pouring their resources into the bottomless pit of seeking security in riches. They are then free to give alms to the poor.

People are not free to help the poor because they believe they need all their wealth to ensure their own security. The sin of the man who planned bigger barns is similar to the sin of the man who hid his talent in the ground (Matt 26.14–30). Their strategy was based on self-centred fear. The sin for which 'bigger barns' is condemned is not his concern for material things. Jesus affirms that God knows we need food and clothes. The rich fool did not care for the poor, because he was anxious to ensure that he had bigger barns in which to store all his goods so that he could enjoy life. If such a person is counselled to share with the poor, the real hurdle he/she must overcome is anxiety about personal security. Jesus equates giving alms to the poor with providing treasure in heaven. Paul does the same in 1 Timothy 6.7–10. Giving alms to the poor was the dominant form of social relief in Jesus' time. Thus those who invest their time and their resources in activity which benefits the poorest, who are showing compassion in a world which only thinks of winners and losers, where people are in slavery to greed or fear, according to Jesus, will reap treasure in heaven. Treasure in heaven is using resources to enable the poor to have their full place in society. Earthly treasures are of use in the kingdom.

Good News for the Rich

This is good news for the rich. Jesus sets them free from rebelling against God by seeking security in their wealth; this expresses no trust in God because riches are being laid up for the self. Jesus sets people free to devote their attention and wealth to the concerns of God's kingdom, God's right relationships, and especially the poor. This new basis for their identity and security as good news to the rich derives in part from the meaning of the good news to the poor which gives the poor a new identity. Rich and poor experience this new identity together because both have been accepted in grace at the cross of Christ. When this understanding is lacking, a process sets in of blaming and fearing others and ignoring the sins in their own communities which contribute to the problem.

Christ's atoning death needs to be central as the basis of forgiveness. God has forgiven us all an unpayable debt so that we may forgive the debts we owe one another. If a sense of Christ's death is not present, people cannot easily let go of the sense of the wrongs they have suffered or that they have been party to inflicting on others. Victims continuously present themselves as victims. They take on an heroic, even messianic role. A competition emerges to demonstrate that one particular group is undergoing the worst suffering. The guilty have continually to express their guilt and atone for it by keeping silent or by a self-righteous posturing on behalf of the oppressed.

Christian organizations engaged in ministry with the poor can be signs of the new identity that God gives the poor and the rich as they serve as partners that express the new sharing in one community between people divided by one of the major causes of division in society—mammon. Organizations such as Traidcraft provide a mechanism by which those with resources can use them to assist the poor to fulfil their human potential and calling to be stewards. Surveys of purchasers of Traidcraft products show them to be predominantly located among middle-class people, and within England in the Southern and Eastern half of the country. They can afford the premium price of fair trade products. The process links such people in a partnership that gives the poor producers a market, and enables people who by any global standard are 'rich' to enter into a trading relationship which questions many of the assumptions of their own culture.

5

Why a Christian Organization?

Assisting poor people to fulfil their calling to be stewards, through a mechanism of trade conducted in accord with principles of justice, in a process that provides a link between poor and non-poor and provide loans to poor people, depends on a particular view of humanity. This view sees human beings as more than objects of charity, human relations as defined by more than economics and the division between human communities brought by mammon as an evil power that holds people in its grip which can only be fully addressed by the cross of Christ that overcomes such evil and such divisions. It sees human rights as applicable to the community relationships of people and the differences between people and groups as occasions for working in partnership rather than divisions to be overcome through conflict.

Many beyond the Christian community share such a view. This happens because on a Christian view the one place where we see evil overcome in the world is the cross of Christ. Therefore any activity or action that expresses the victory of good over evil, and takes forward the forces of life over against the forces of darkness, is ultimately attributable to Christ's victory over evil on the cross. Those who work to forward the well-being of humanity without consciously acknowledging the source or goal of life are nevertheless able to make their contribution because of what the cross of Christ has achieved. The witness of Christian partnership to them is to point to the source, empowerment and goal of such a process which more often than not will become a relevant issue somewhere along the line.

But some will question the basis for such a view of humanity. It is here that the inextricable link between religion and assisting poor people is seen. First, a religious view of the world is inevitably involved when discussing the nature and identity of human beings. Secondly, the world is continually relearning, often at great cost, the link between religion and morality. In September 1998 with colleagues from around the world I visited Vukovar, the Croatian city on the borders of Serbia. Vukovar had been besieged and taken by Serbian forces during the civil war. It was handed back to Croatia in January 1998. It had been devastated. 12,000 of its population of 60,000 had been killed. In a powerful speech the President of the District spoke of their pledge to reshape their education system. She said they had been brought to this pass through 70 years of a system that divorced religion and morality. As a result people had neither respected ties of family nor humanity in the awful slaughter. They were therefore committed to raising the next generation to understand the religious roots of human morality.

Thirdly, most poor people in the world are religious and relate their situation in some way to religion. They are often more open to work with and trust people who make a religious commitment than those of whose commitments they are unsure.

Fourthly, a Christian approach to assisting poor people should not act in a form of practical welfarism, as though economics dictated everything in life. On the contrary, those working in development have time and again discovered that a fundamental issue for poor people is who they are. Their religious societies tell them they are defiled and cursed; economic comparisons tell them they are losers. The Christian gospel tells them that they are created as stewards of God and called to be his children through grace, despite their supposed demerits. The greatest evidence for this is the cross of Christ which brings the good news that victory over all opposing and evil powers has been won. Part of the culture of poor people, which enables them to cope psychologically with the harshness of their existence, is that it is their fate—that they are paying a price for somebody's action somewhere. In religious terms it may be a price for the past sins of their family, or in anticipation of future blessedness. In secular terms it may be the price for past structural oppression, or in anticipation of national economic recovery. This reinforces in the poor a sense of victimization at the hands of forces they cannot control. They attribute to these forces enormous power before which they are helpless. Thus fate also stifles creativity and responsibility. This false consciousness is an expression of sin and death that destroys God's purpose for life.

The Price Paid

The atonement announces that the price is already paid for the past and that the price of the future is secured. This releases in people a new sense of identity. They are somebody. By grace they are not damnable and useless people. They are called to be sons and daughters of God, to be friends of Jesus, to be inheritors of the promises of God and in the church to be the bride of Christ. As his creation they are called to have dominion over the earth and are accountable to him. As his children they are restored to this position despite their supposed and real demerits, because of the cross. Indwelt by God's Spirit, they have access to the power of God through prayer, to the armoury of God against evil, and to the resources of God which are far more than material. This is true empowerment.

18

The forces of the global market economy marginalize religion. For the wealthy of the world to deny poor people not only access to economic resources but also to deny the reality of the world of religion which gives an alternative basis for identity to that which is defined by the rich, is a double deprivation. Christian involvement to assist poor people may not always be religious in expression. But it is necessarily religious in foundation as this is a powerful alternative basis from which to challenge the definitions and frameworks the wealthy put on the world. These definitions and frameworks are constantly changing. A Christian response to them needs to be constantly updated. Over the last fifty years the predominant western Christian response to poverty has moved, where it has gone beyond indifference, from provision of welfare, to involvement in nation-building, to building community awareness and education, to trade and micro-credit enterprise. We cannot assume we have reached the final and sufficient solution. There will be new challenges and new responses. We are already seeing ideas of fair trade and small scale business development being taken up by supermarket chains (B&Q) and world organizations (World Bank). In this we rejoice. But in the process they will be open to misuse and abuse. A Christian organization must also constantly review its own analysis of problems and advocacy of solutions in the light of God's revealed will in Scripture. It must also recognize that Christian values are to be rooted in and resourced by a living relationship with Jesus Christ. The traditions of humanitarianism, however worthy, will not be adequate on their own.

Thus Christian faith-based organizations have an important place in the field of assistance to the poor. This is not just because the poor need to hear the gospel. The poor need an approach to dealing with the problems of poverty and enabling them to obtain true humanity which constantly seeks to maintain the quality of God's will for human beings. Such an approach must address the oppressive structures of world trade, seek to enable poor people to develop their own entrepreneurial skills and believe them to be worthy of credit and to receive loans. It must see a role for the non-poor in addressing their situation, enable the poor to build their families and their communities and see the importance of fair wages and reward. It must provide space for compassionate action, speak to governments about the poor of the earth, work for benefits to communities and address the divisions between people caused by mammon. All these components are rooted in a biblical understanding of human beings as created persons in community, called to be stewards in a world where evil has been overcome in the cross of Christ.

Thomas Jeavons' study *When the Bottom Line is Faithfulness* classifies Christian organizations as either the faith-based organization or the faith-promoting organization.[19] The faith-based organization seeks to live out the implications of the Christian faith. Jeavons specifies a number of assumptions underlying its culture:

---

19 Thomas Jeavons, *When the Bottom Line is Faithfulness: Management of Christian Service Organizations* (Indiana University Press, 1994).

- It perceives its work as a ministry.
- It cares for practical and spiritual needs as one.
- It sees itself as part of the church and serves a specific Christian constituency.
- It believes that God will provide the resources for his work. Fundraising is not an end in itself.
- To serve and care for each other in the organization is regarded as important as service and care for others.
- It is maintained by two factors—the commitment of the founders and the recruitment policy of the organization.

The impact of a Christian organization depends not only on its activity but also on its witness, how it engages in its activity, the care it exercises for its own members, the example it sets, the encouragement it gives, the inspiration it provides and the space it creates in society to say 'The market place is not just a place of relative winners and losers, where there are gains from trade for all, but they are shared unequally. You can be just and loving, and care better for people and the environment, as you compete in the market place of fair trade.' The impact it has depends not only on the outcomes, but also on the space that this and other Christian organizations create in society for the values and commitments they stand for.

Fair Trade in the Future

Christian Fair Trade organizations can show the frontier of the kingdom of God with the current economic order; enable people to become stewards of creation; can be a parable that changes people one step at a time, but irrevocably; and an event that can give opportunity for an explanation that is rooted in why we believe justice is so fundamental and why we believe that action for justice is not in vain.

Christian good news must be good for the poor. So does Fair Trade really help the poor? Professor Deryke Belshaw, for many years a trustee of the Traidcraft Foundation, argues: 'Injecting welfare into competitive international commodity markets raises costs and is self-defeating. Thus the Fair Trade organization is non-sustainable unless (1) consumers are willing to pay more; (2) the margins of middle-men (retailers and agents) are cut; (3) management is paid less; and/or (4) all competitors are required by law to observe minimum standards; (5) all imports into industrial countries from low income countries are liable to tax (ATOs would show grounds for exemption) and proceeds transferred to low income countries.'

ATOs need to be clear about which mechanism they use and how these are justified. Thus Traidcraft has used mechanisms 1, 2 and 3. Direct sales of fairly traded commodities through mainstream outlets (CafeDirect and TeaDirect, the FairTrade mark) rely on mechanism 1 only. Mechanisms 4 and 5 raise bureaucratic costs and may substitute industrialized governments' actions for two-thirds world governments' actions or become a substitute for aid. Poorer consumers may not be able to pay the premium suggested in mechanism 1. This actually is reflected in Traidcraft's consumer profile.

A price premium can be seen as a form of charity which is a biblical principle. It represents an attempt to provide income support through well rewarded work by people assuming a neighbourly responsibility to enable those on hard times to take their place again in the community and exercise their calling to be stewards. Is buying something a little more expensive a gesture of willingness to assist and accept responsibility for changing unfair systems?

The market for fairly traded products is new and dynamic; ideas about how to promote fair trade effectively are changing. Some argue that given a high ATO price premium, non-ATO competition will enter the market offering the same 'fairly-traded' benefits at a lower price. If these claims are accurate (and an independent and compulsory standards mechanism would seem necessary here), the central task of the original ATOs may be completed. But there is scope for greater efficiency, such as each ATO sourcing other ATOs to achieve economies of scale, and for additional activities, such as analysing and critiquing international trade or environmental legislation and practices which disadvantage poor producers. Promoting minimum standards in business and trade are likely to become more significant in ensuring fair trade in the future. The activity of marketing fairly traded goods as a business is fundamental to this in demonstrating that business can be done ethically in ways that benefit poor producers.

Does Traidcraft Need to be a Christian Organization to Fight Poverty Through Trade?

Traidcraft focuses upon the development of trade and small businesses as an expression of Christian mission with particular ethical values as paramount. Why are these values chosen and made paramount? They are compatible with a vision of humanity which is founded in and expressed in a Christian experience and view which we believe is true.

The source and support for these values is a living relationship with Jesus Christ. We speak of values but they have no separate existence as absolutes. The reality of the world for Christians is that it is created for and will be fulfilled in the lordship of Christ over everything. When he returns he will establish a reign of justice and peace. Prior to his return this reign is exercised through the active rule of the kingdom of God which is present in quality but not full quantity. Many aspects of this reign find an echo in the concerns and aspirations of people who are not Christian. This is to be expected since the kingdom of God is the fulfilment of creation, and experience of life in creation often, but not always, gives rise to many of the values that find full expression in the kingdom of God.

However, these values are not static. They always need to re-express full humanity in Jesus in ways that accurately speak to contemporary life. Christians are rightly selective in choosing which challenges to pursue. Many developments in the world are to be resisted in the name of full humanity. But some are to be embraced. There is a distinct tendency to legalism in any prophetic movement—

witness for example the excesses of eco-fascists. It is very important that Traidcraft does not become legalistic or think that it has a blueprint.

Can Poverty Be More Effectively Fought Through a Christian Organization?
    The argument about effectiveness requires a judgment of history. In nineteenth century India Christian mission among the outcast groups (Dalits) was highly effective in enabling them to develop out of poverty. And a recent study done in Latin America shows that the Pentecostals have had astounding success in enabling people to take responsibility for their work and families and move themselves up and out of degrading poverty.[20]
    To answer the question brings us to the role of Christian faith in addressing poverty. Christian faith makes a difference to the understanding of poverty. Poverty cannot be reduced solely to matters of economics and international trade, however significant these may be. Many dimensions of poverty, such as enforced low self-esteem, greed and corruption are directly addressed by the gospel of Jesus. There is the whole culture of poverty—the belief of many poor people that they deserve their poverty, that it is a punishment for past wrongdoing, or that it is their fate in some way. The good news of the gospel is that Christ has died to overcome fate and any forces that they may believe are working against them. In Christ, those who are made to feel by the systems of the world that they are nothing and worthless can through grace become sons and daughters of God. They gain a new identity. They are called and enabled to be stewards of his creation.
    No secular development organization or Government agency can bring about this wider self-understanding which is so important for the development of people's motivation and effort to change their lives and take responsibility for their families. That is why the gospel and the building up of the church are so vital for addressing poverty. Traidcraft has focused very specifically on building up the ability of communities to trade on equal terms. It is important that local churches should know of the links Traidcraft has with producer organizations in their locality. Of course, all Christians and their institutions need to be open to identifying and learning from errors and gaps in their actions and to institute methods for accelerating these processes. Therefore, the work of Traidcraft forms one part, but only one part, of a holistic Christian response. Traidcraft focuses on fighting poverty through trade not because it believes that that is the only or best way to fight poverty. It recognizes that it is an essential part of a multisectoral and holistic approach in a globalized economy.

2 0 Jorge Maldonado 'Building Fundamentalism from the family in Latin America' in *Fundamentalism and Society*, Martin Marty and R Scott Appleby (eds) (Chicago University Press, 1993) pp 214–239.

6
Bibliography

Fair Trade

Adams, R, *Who Profits? A Revealing Case Study in Successful Trading with Developing Countries* (Oxford: Lion, 1989)

Adams, R; Carruthers, J; Fisher, C, *Shopping for a Better World: A Quick and Easy Guide to Socially Responsible Shopping* (London: Kogan Page Ltd, 1991)

Adams, R; Wells, P; Webb, I, *For a Better World: A Social Action Guide for Christians* (Oxford: Lynx, 1994)

Barratt Brown, M, *Fair Trade: Reform and Realities in the International Trading System* (London: Zed Books, 1993)

Burns, S, *Fair Trade: a Rough Guide for Business* (London: TWIN, 1996)

Cho, G, *Trade and Global Interdependence* (London: Routledge, 1995)

Coote, B, *The Trade Trap: Poverty and The Global Commodity Markets* (Oxford: Oxfam 1992)

Davenport, M; Page, S, *World Trade Reform: Do Developing Countries Win or Lose?* (London: ODI, 1994)

Dobson, A, *Green Political Thought* (London: Routledge, 1995)

EFTA Fair Trade Yearbook (Maastricht, Netherlands: European Fair Trade Association, 1995)

Ekins, P, *A New World Order: Grass Roots Movements for Social Change* (London: Routledge, 1992)

Goldsmith, J, *The Response: Gatt and Global Free Trade* (London: Macmillan, 1995)

Madden, P, *A Raw Deal: Trade and the World's Poor* (London: Christian Aid, 1992)

Madeley, J, *Trade and the Poor: The Impact of International Trade on Developing Countries* (London: Intermediate Technology Publications, 1992)

ODA 'Microfinance is now big Business' Internet Article http://www.oneworld.org/oda/publications/bod47/business.html

Page, S, *How Developing Countries Trade* (London: Routledge, 1994)

Sugden, J, *Is there a Fair Trade Model that can be Extended to International Trade at a Macro-Level?* (Durham University Dissertation in Social Sciences, 1997)

Vallely, P, *Promised Lands: Stories of Power and Poverty in the Third World* (London: Fount and Christian Aid, 1992)

Christian Mission and the Poor

Bussau, D, *Reflections on Christian Microenterprise Development* (Opportunity International, 103 High Street, Oxford, 1999)

Bussau, D and Samuel, V, *How then should we lend? A Biblical Validation of Microenterprise Development* (Opportunity International, 1999)

Orlando Costas, *Liberating News* (Grand Rapids: Eerdmans, 1989)

de Santa Ana, J, *Good News to the Poor* (Geneva: WCC, 1977)

Fung, R, 'Good News to the Poor—a case for a missionary movement' in *Your Kingdom Come* (Geneva: WCC, 1980)

Hall, D, *The Steward—a Biblical Symbol Come of Age* (New York: Friendship Press, 1982)

Houston, T, 'Good News for the Poor' in *Transformation*, January 1990

Mason, J, 'Biblical Teaching and Assisting the Poor' in *Transformation*, April 1987

Petersen, D, *Not by Might nor by Power* (Oxford: Regnum, 1996)

Samuel, V and C, 'Rebuilding Families—a Priority for Wholistic Mission' in *Transformation* Vol 9, No 3, July 1993

Samuel,V; Sugden, C, *Evangelism and the Poor* (Carlisle: Paternoster, 1983) pp 37–106

Sarracco, N, 'The Liberating Options of Jesus' in *Sharing Jesus in the Two Thirds World*, edited by Samuel, V and Sugden, C (Grand Rapids: Eerdmans, 1986)

Schlossberg, H, Samuel, V and Sider, R J, *Christianity and Economics in the Post-Cold War Era* (Grand Rapids: Eerdmans, 1994)

Sider, R J, *Rich Christians in an Age of Hunger* (Hodder and Stoughton, 1978) chapters 3–5

Sider, R J, *Evangelism and Social Action* (Hodder and Stoughton, 1993) Appendix 'Is Social Justice Part of Salvation?'

Sider, R J, *Cup of Water, Bread of Life* (Grand Rapids: Zondervan, 1994)

Sugden, C, 'Poverty' in *New Dictionary of Theology* edited by A Ferguson and C Wright (Leicester: Inter Varsity Press, 1988)

Sugden, C 'What is Good about Good News to the Poor?' In *AD 2000 and Beyond—A Mission Agenda* edited by Samuel, V and Sugden, C (Oxford: Regnum, 1991)

Sugden, C and Barclay, O, *Kingdom and Creation in Social Ethics* (Grove Ethical Study 79, 1990)

Sugden, C, *Seeking The Asian Face of Jesus* (Oxford: Regnum, 1997) chapter 10—section on Mission and Development

Sugden, C, 'Jesus Christ, Saviour and Liberator' in Nicholls, B and Wood, B (eds) *Sharing Good News with the Poor* (Carlisle: Paternoster, 1996)

'Charity which gives nothing away' in *Christian Action Journal*, Autumn 1993

'Children at Risk,' in *Transformation*, April 1997

'A Christian Response to Disability' in *Transformation*, October 1998

'Oxford Declaration on Christian Faith and Economics' in *Transformation*, April 1990

Traidcraft, Kingsway, Team Valley, Newcastle upon Tyne NE11 0NE.
Tel: 0191 491 0591. Web: http://www.traidcraft.co.uk

Share Interest, 25 Collingwood Street, Newcastle upon Tyne NE1 1JE.
Tel: 0191 233 9100. Web: http://www.shared-interest.com